Henley in the Age of Enlightenment

Introducing
The Rev. Humphrey Gainsborough
&
personalities who contributed to the blossoming of the arts and sciences

based on the Special Exhibition

Genius & Gentility
at the
**River & Rowing Museum
26 January – 15 September, 2002**

Roger Kendal   Jane Bowen   Laura Wortley

Henley in the Age of Enlightenment

Foreword by The Lord Camoys

The eighteenth century is often referred to as 'The Age of Enlightenment'. Writers and philosophers of the period thought that they were emerging from centuries of darkness into a new age of reason that challenged accepted beliefs and encouraged free thought. This period of creativity across Europe led to a blossoming of the arts and sciences that was mirrored in the small town of Henley-on-Thames in Oxfordshire. Here, among the families of the nobility, gentry and clergy, scientific ideas were discussed and developed, literary works were written and fashionable new designs for their houses and gardens were implemented.

Research into the achievements of this fascinating group of people inspired the River & Rowing Museum to present the special exhibition 'Genius & Gentility' in 2002.

Publication of this book, which adds more information about the characters involved and includes first-hand accounts of their everyday lives from the diaries and journals of Caroline Powys, was made possible by the generous sponsorship of Sir Harry Djanogly.

The talents of some of the most famous designers of the time, including James Wyatt and Capability Brown were employed by local landowners. The leading artist, Thomas Gainsborough painted portraits of the Conway family of Park Place. Anne Damer, General Conway's only daughter, became widely known as an artist and sculptress whose works can still be seen on Henley Bridge and at Fawley Court.

At the same time a small group of innovative men, including the nonconformist minister Humphrey Gainsborough, brother of Thomas Gainsborough, was experimenting with new ideas that resulted in practical improvements in engineering and agricultural equipment. For many years he remained an unrecognised genius. This book highlights his work and commends the industry and artistic achievements of all these colourful local characters that embody the theme of the original special exhibition 'Genius and Gentility'.

Henley in the 18th Century

In 1750, Henley-on-Thames in Oxfordshire was a small town of about 3500 inhabitants with a thriving market and riverside wharf where timber, firewood and grain were despatched to London. It had not changed significantly from the view of the town painted by Jan Siberechts in 1698.

Henley from the Wargrave Road, 1698 by Jan Siberechts

This painting clearly shows the old wooden bridge, damaged in 1642 during the Civil War, the tower of St Mary's Church and the River Thames with numerous barges transporting local produce downstream to London and returning with luxury goods for the country houses of the wealthy gentry. Malting grain before it was transported to London was still one of the most important local trades, as it had been in 1705 when it was described in detail by Doctor Robert Plot in the second edition of the Natural History of Oxfordshire. There were a number of small local breweries providing beer, part of the staple diet of local inhabitants and the itinerant teams of hauliers who towed barges upstream.

In the 1750s, Henley still had two rows of shambles in the town centre, known as Butcher Row and Fisher Row, near the old Guildhall, that was finally demolished in 1781. The town had also started to expand along Friday Street and the Reading Road, into the parish of Rotherfield Greys, including a new chapel for the Independent Congregation built in 1719 near the site of the old barn seen in the Siberechts' painting.

Prosperity and Politics

The eighteenth century was a period of relative stability in England after the political, economic and religious upheavals that had followed the Civil War. Georgian England was prosperous and more of the landowning gentry made a 'Grand Tour' of Europe to see the remains of classical civilizations. Gentlemen met in coffee houses to conduct business or exchange ideas and this led to the formation of societies where discussion could be held without the censure of religious or class division. For the first time men mixed with others from different levels of society, who would normally be outside their immediate circle of family and friends. Meanwhile, the engineering practices and mechanical inventions that heralded the Industrial Revolution were being developed.

View of Henley upon Thames

J. Buckler, 1789

This view, looking down Hart Street towards St. Mary's Church and the newly constructed stone bridge, clearly shows the wide street that formed the original market area for goods destined for London. A section of the churchyard, together with the almshouses, had recently been removed to provide better access to the new bridge opened in 1786.

Henley in the Age of Enlightenment

An Election I: An Entertainment
Engraving after a painting by William Hogarth
The rival Whig and Tory parties sought to influence eligible voters with lavish dinners and entertainment. A Whig 'treat' is depicted here, with all manner of debauchery, whilst a mob in the pay of the Tory opposition attempts to batter down the doors.

We know very little about 90% of the population of this time. They were not listed as electors and there are few written records that give us an insight into their daily lives. Church records, land transactions, apprentice indentures and court records tell us some of their names, ages and occupations. These ranged from innkeepers, tradesmen and shopkeepers to menial servants, agricultural labourers and those who subsisted by working for others. Often the whole family worked together, making it impossible for the children to go to school. The poorest were frequently described as *"idle, disorderly and supported by criminal delinquency."* Charity was only given to the fortunate few, so illness, unemployment or lack of family support could quickly reduce anyone to the lowest level. The top 2% of the population, the nobility and country gentlemen who owned nearly all the land, controlled the wealth of the nation. Only men, known as forty-shilling freeholders because they owned sufficient land, were able to vote. These included some clergy and wealthy professionals such as lawyers, doctors and bankers as well as ship owners, merchants, manufacturers, shopkeepers, artists, builders and mechanics. In Henley, only 148 men were registered electors and many of them were not resident in the parish.

The General Election of 1754, called by the ruling Whig party, was the first since 1715. The two Tory Members of Parliament for Oxfordshire had been unopposed since 1710. They represented the Established Church, sympathised with local squires and landowners and their enemies accused them of involvement in the Jacobite Rebellion of 1745. They were opposed in 1754 by two Whig candidates who had links with the City of London and were more sympathetic to mercantile interests and Protestant dissenters. The election in Oxfordshire was notoriously corrupt and inspired William Hogarth to produce a series of etchings exposing the bribes offered by the candidates in the form of 'treats' where voters were invited to eat and drink to excess, fighting between rival factions and vote rigging.

There is no evidence that this political rivalry had a lasting effect on Henley society where discussion flourished between men from different social and religious backgrounds due to shared interests in science and engineering.

An Election III: The Polling
Engraving after a painting by William Hogarth
There was no secret ballot and voters were often required to swear to their eligibility. Here one man is shown voting under direction and a soldier who is unable to hold the Bible because he has lost his hands, is causing a legal argument about his ability to swear the oath.

The Social Hierarchy

A strict hierarchy was obvious at all social gatherings. The Royal family and the titled gentry were the accepted leaders of society, but it was possible for successful men to move up the social scale and become country gentlemen by acquiring wealth and property through patronage, marriage, intellectual ability or fortunate investments. Similarly, at a lower level, respectable traders could also rise to the level of minor gentry.

The Established Church and Dissenters

Antagonism towards the extreme religious beliefs held by many of those who opposed Charles I had resulted in persecution of Nonconformist congregations after the Restoration of Charles II in 1660. A more tolerant attitude to religion led to the relaxation of this legislation early in the eighteenth century, but nonconformists were still not allowed to attend established Universities and marriages were not permitted in their chapels until late in the nineteenth century.

Catholics had also been subjected to persecution for their beliefs from the reign of Elizabeth I. They were fined for not attending church services and could be executed for harbouring priests. The unsuccessful attempts to restore the Stuart monarchy in 1715 and 1745 reinforced the legislation against Catholics who were viewed with great suspicion.

Despite the legislation, both Nonconformist and Catholic dissenters appear to have been accepted in Henley society.

Park Place
"...it possesses a grandeur of composition which is not seen elsewhere on the river it adorns." Boydell, 1793

During his estrangement from his father, King George II, Frederick Prince of Wales lived at Park Place from 1738 until 1751. After his death, General Henry Seymour Conway purchased Park Place. As the second son of Lord Conway, he was ensured a superior position in local society above Sambrooke Freeman and his nephew Strickland Freeman who, although they were Lords of the Manor of Henley and Remenham and lived in the fine mansion of Fawley Court, were untitled gentry.

Gentlemen and their families from the country estates around Henley would meet at parties and dine at each other's houses. Some were relative newcomers to the area and others long established but nearly all followed the established faith of the Church of England. Two notable exceptions were the Stonor and Hall families.

The long established and aristocratic Stonor family, who held extensive lands in the area, were unable to play their full role in society because of their adherence to the Catholic faith, but they were included in local society parties and the Henley Gala Week of 1777. Also present was Thomas Hall of Harpsden Court, who had inherited the estate from his father. Both his father and grandfather had attended Oxford University (which required all students to be members of the established church) and had become lawyers at the Middle Temple. He appears to have been the first generation of his family to become a country gentleman. Relatively little is known about the Hall family, as their archives were lost in the Blitz during WW2, but surviving Henley documents reveal Hall's nonconformist views on religion and his support for the Independent Congregation in Henley including his friendship with the minister Humphrey Gainsborough.

The wealthy families, who made up the top 2% of society, relied on the skill and ingenuity of qualified professionals and the artistic ability of the craftsmen who designed, decorated and improved their country houses, landscaped their estates, painted their portraits and supplied them with fine clothes and luxury goods. However there was a fine line drawn between those considered their equals with whom they would socialise and those they employed. Many of the latter, including artists, designers and furniture makers, are now more famous than their original clients. Information about the daily lives of many of these people has survived in family archives, diaries, letters, business accounts and sometimes in portraits.

Field Marshal Henry Seymour Conway of Park Place
By Thomas Gainsborough, 1780

People and Places

General Henry Seymour Conway of Park Place

> *"England has a Conway, the power of whose eloquence, inspired by his zeal for liberty, animated with the fire of true genius, and furnished with sound knowledge of the constitution, at once entertain, ravish, convince, conquer."*
>
> Letter to 'The Cocoa Tree' from Albermarle Street 1764/5.

Henry Seymour Conway (1721 – 1795) was the second son of Lord Conway and brother of the 1st Marquis of Hertford. He bought Park Place from the estate of Frederick, Prince of Wales in 1752. A Member of Parliament from 1747 to 1784, he was a government minister from 1764 to 1768 and worked with William Pitt the Elder. At the same time he pursued his military career and was Governor of Jersey in the 1780s. David Hume, one of the leading philosophers of the 18th century, worked as his private secretary. He and his family played an active part in London's aristocratic and artistic society and were particularly interested in the theatre. Conway was a friend of David Garrick who produced his play 'False Appearances' at the Theatre Royal, Drury Lane in 1789. He was also a prominent figure in local affairs, serving as a Thames Commissioner and involved with the local Turnpike Trust. As a member of the Henley Bridge Commissioners, who undertook the supervision of the design and building of a new bridge in the 1780s, Conway's ideas on improvements to the curve of the central arch of the bridge were incorporated into the final design.

Turnpike Trusts

The growth of traffic in the 17th century made road surfaces so bad that they could no longer be adequately maintained by the parishes responsible for them. This led to the introduction of Turnpike Trusts, local groups set up by Act of Parliament, to collect tolls from road users in order to pay interest on money borrowed for the maintenance and development of specified stretches of road. The name 'Turnpike' arose because the toll bar, placed across the road to halt traffic, resembled a soldier's pike. A typical trust consisted of a surveyor, a local lawyer as clerk, and the local landowners whose property lay alongside the road. Tolls were set for each category of road user, wagons at first being charged by size, but since it was heavier loads that caused most damage to roads, they were later charged by weight.

Weighing machines were built at strategic points near the turnpike gates to provide a certified weight for each load. The first trust was set up in 1663, but most were launched in the 18th century.

There were three turnpike trusts in the Henley area:-

The Henley – Bix – Dorchester Turnpike Trust set up in 1736
The Reading – Henley – Hatfield Turnpike Trust set up in 1768
The Henley – Hurley Turnpike Trust. The earliest records of this trust are lost, but later references show that it was in operation by 1768, when the first improvements to White Hill took place. As significant landowners along the route, General Conway and Sambrooke Freeman would have been key members of the trust.

Henley in the Age of Enlightenment

> *"The arch was regulated by General Conway himself, on three centres, and for grace does not vail the bonnet to the Ponte di Trinita, at Florence."* Horace Walpole, 1785.

Like many landowners of the time, Conway devoted much time, energy and money to the 'improvement' of his country estate. His many alterations, some incorporating Lady Ailesbury's designs, transformed it into an elegant setting for social gatherings. In 1768, he employed the Reverend Humphrey Gainsborough on the vast engineering project that reduced the slope of White Hill. This not only made the approach to Henley from London less hazardous but also drew traffic away from the easier route through the grounds of Park Place.

The estate was extensively landscaped, largely to Conway's own designs, producing beautiful terraces overlooking the Thames and Henley. An underground passage led down to 'Happy Valley' where the architect, James 'Athenian' Stuart, built a classical ruin. He involved Humphrey Gainsborough in the construction of 'Conway's Bridge' over this valley in 1763, using stones from the ruined Reading Abbey. This bridge still carries the main road from Wargrave to Henley. Later, the 'Druids' Temple', a gift from the grateful people of Jersey, was erected in the grounds in 1788.

Conway was also personally involved in scientific developments and became a member of the Society for the encouragement of the Arts, Manufactures and Science in 1764. In the 1770s he began growing lavender at Park Place and installed a distillation plant at the property now known as 'Woodlands' to produce lavender oil. This scheme provided seasonal work for local people, but also enabled him to experiment with the distillation of other plant liquids and develop furnace designs and coking processes for which he was awarded patents in 1782 and 1789. He promoted the idea of using waste heat from the processes, an idea that was used in the 20th century for district heating projects linked to power stations.

Henry Seymour Conway as a young man

People and Places

Lady Caroline Ailesbury

> "The noble Countess of Aylesbury [sic] whose imitations of Cuyp, Rosa de Tivoli, Vandyck, Gainsborough, &c in needlework, are little inferior in effect to their originals..."
>
> 'Picturesque Views of the River Thames', 1792 Samuel Ireland.

In 1747 Conway married the widow Caroline, Countess of Ailesbury, the daughter of Lt. General John Campbell (later Duke of Argyll). They had one daughter Anne born in 1749. Caroline was a renowned society hostess and needlework artist, who was devoted to the theatre. An accomplished artistic designer, she advised Horace Walpole on the décor of his house at Strawberry Hill. After Conway's death in 1795 she sold Park Place and lived with Anne at Strawberry Hill. She died in 1811 and was buried at Sundridge, Kent, in a tomb designed by her daughter.

Lady Ailesbury's Aviary from Mrs. Powys' sketchbook

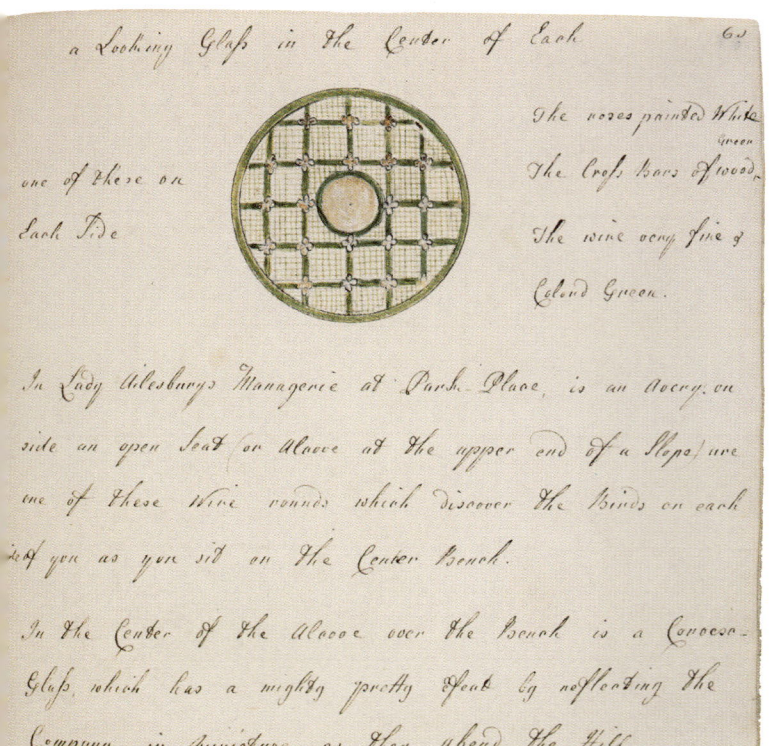

Mrs Anne Seymour Damer

Anne, the only daughter of General Conway and Lady Ailesbury, lived from 1749 to 1828.

In 1767 she married John Damer, son of Lord Milton. This unhappy marriage ended when he committed suicide in 1776 after incurring huge gambling debts at the card tables.

Miniature of Anne Damer by Jeremiah Meyer, R.A.

Well travelled and educated, Anne was a friend of Georgiana, Duchess of Devonshire, and became a leading member of her 'Devonshire House Circle', which included Garrick and the playwright Sheridan in its ranks. She is reputed to have been the first woman in England to wear black silk stockings.

*"Long with soft touch shall Damer's chisel charm
With grace delight and with beauty warm"*

Lady Melbourne

Horace Walpole, a cousin of her father Henry Conway, ensured that her early education was broadly based. She inherited a life interest in Strawberry Hill after his death. Whilst a young woman, she travelled widely and received tuition in sculpture from Ceracchi, who modelled his statue of The Muse of Sculpture on her. As an accomplished sculptress in an age when women artists were few, she often received unfavourable comments from professional artists. She was an Honorary Exhibitor at the Royal Academy in London, showing over thirty sculptures there between 1784 and 1818. In 1802 she gave one of her works, a bust of Charles James Fox, to Napoleon and in return he presented her with a diamond-encrusted snuff box which is now in the British Museum.

In 1785 she exhibited at the Royal Academy in London reliefs in terracotta and plaster of Isis and Tamesis, which were carved in stone for the keystones of the central arch of the new Henley Bridge. She was also a skilled designer and examples of her work can be seen at Fawley Court where she produced classical decorations for Sambrooke Freeman's library.

In later life her mannish dress and devotion to Miss Berry was publicly criticised. It is therefore not surprising that her novel 'Belmour', was published anonymously in 1801. She also acted in and produced plays with her aristocratic friends, where her efforts were highly praised.

Isis and Tamesis by Anne Seymour Damer

Terracotta and plaster, exhibited at the Royal Academy in 1785 (nos. 591, 592)

People and Places

Sambrooke Freeman of Fawley Court

William Freeman purchased the Fawley Court estate in 1679 and rebuilt the house in Wren style in 1684. The family became wealthy through trading with the East India Company and slave trading between Africa and the West Indies. Sambrooke Freeman inherited Fawley Court from his father in 1757. His education had included travelling in Italy and this encouraged an early interest in classical art, architecture and the landscape. He even wrote to the Royal Society in 1750 about his visit to Pompeii.

In 1768 he purchased Phyllis Court, together with the manors of Henley and Remenham and carried out extensive alterations to Fawley Court incorporating many of his own architectural ideas. These were much admired by Mrs Lybbe Powys who recorded them in her diary. In the library he installed a wooden frieze and panels designed by Mrs Anne Damer, a friend of the family. He purchased classical statues including a cast of the Farnese Venus to enhance the property. Capability Brown landscaped the grounds around the house and James Wyatt added the Temple on the island in the Thames in 1771, including interior decorations based on figures from classical vases in the British Museum.

Sambrooke joined the Society of Arts in 1756, only two years after its foundation and encouraged both Thomas Powys and Humphrey Gainsborough to contact the Society with their ideas. On his death in 1782, his nephew Strickland Freeman inherited Fawley Court.

Fawley Court as seen from the Thames after the addition of white stucco in 1787, with landscaping by Capability Brown.

From the sketch book of Caroline Powys.

The Temple on the Island designed by James Wyatt in 1771 and the gothic-style folly near the house.

> The first meeting of the 'Society for the encouragement of the Arts, Manufactures and Science' took place at Rawthmell's Coffee House, Covent Garden in 1754. The Society offered premiums to promote improvements in Agriculture, Chemistry, Colonies & Trade, Manufactures, Mechanics and the Polite Arts. The name had been contracted to the 'Society of Arts' by 1783 and it received the title 'Royal' in 1908.

The Reverend Thomas Powys

> "...a most genial able man, a great favourite in society and a remarkable talent for rhyming"
>
> St John's College, Oxford - 'Biographical Register for 1752/3'

Thomas Powys (1736 – 1809) was the younger brother of Philip Lybbe Powys of Hardwick and, like him, was educated at St John's College, Oxford. He became a Church of England minister and held the posts of Rector of Fawley from 1762, Chaplain to George III from 1781 and by 1797 was Dean of Canterbury. He was a close friend of Sambrooke Freeman and shared his interest in scientific matters, particularly in relation to the sowing of grass seed and the development of good pasture. He wrote at length to the Society of Arts outlining his ideas on the right mix of types of grass to suit different conditions. Despite the difference between their backgrounds and professed religions, he worked closely with

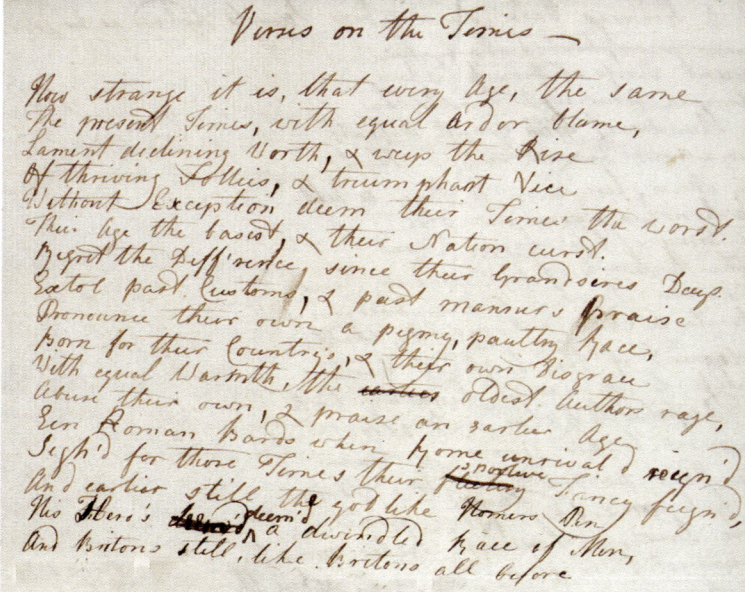

Extract from 'Verses on the Times' by Thomas Powys

the local Independent minister, Humphrey Gainsborough, who developed drill ploughs to enable seed to be sown more consistently than by hand. Thomas wrote in support of Gainsborough's entry when one of these drill ploughs won first prize in a Society of Arts competition in 1765.

Powys was a gentleman and a respected clergyman, which ensured that he was a guest at all the society gatherings. He also played a role in local affairs as a Thames Commissioner and a Henley Bridge Commissioner. He provided employment for the poor in his parish by his grass planting experiments.

Unexpectedly, he was also a prolific poet, writing rhymed verse for all occasions. His compositions included a prologue for each of the plays produced at the Henley Gala in 1777 and a farewell verse for Queen Caroline when he gave up the position of Chaplain to George III to become Dean of Canterbury in 1797.

His elder brother, Philip Lybbe Powys, of Hardwick House near Whitchurch and his wife Caroline were frequent visitors at Fawley Rectory. Through Thomas they became involved in Henley society. Caroline's diaries and sketchbooks provide a valuable insight into eighteenth century life.

Thomas Powys, Dean of Canterbury (1797-1809)
Painting attributed to John Hoppner

People and Places

Thomas Stonor of Stonor Park

View of Stonor House and Chapel

Thomas Stonor (1710 – 1772) was descended from an aristocratic family that had owned extensive estates including Stonor Park since the 12th century. The staunchly Catholic family had suffered confiscation of lands and imposition of recusancy fines from the time of Elizabeth I because they refused to renounce their faith. Thomas Stonor inherited the Stonor estate in 1724, but following the 1745 Jacobite uprising when the Catholic Charles Edward tried to overthrow George II, he found it advisable to keep a low profile and travelled extensively abroad. He returned to live at Stonor in 1753 but handed over responsibility for the estate to his son Charles Stonor in 1762.

During these difficult years the family continued to carry out their duties in the locality, and were welcomed at many local society gatherings. In 1759 Thomas Stonor redecorated the Great Hall at Stonor in the Gothic syle, only nine years after its first appearance at Strawberry Hill.

Anthony Hodges of Bolney Court

The Hodges family moved to Bolney Court in 1746 and bought it eight years later with money from their West Indian plantations. Anthony Hodges (1755 – 1781) maintained links with the Caribbean – *"William Caesar, a black belonging to Anthony Hodges Esq."* was buried at Harpsden on August 13th 1778. His sister Elizabeth Hodges played major roles in both 'The Provok'd Husband' and scenes from 'Pygmalion' that were performed before an audience of 300 in the coach house at Bolney Court and were a key feature of the Henley Gala Week of 1777. Anthony Hodges died in St Kitts in 1781 and was buried in Harpsden churchyard.

*"Buried December 6th 1784
Anthony Hodges Esq. of
Bolney brought from St Kits near three years after his decease"*

Harpsden Church Register

Richard Hayward

Richard Hayward (d. 1797) was a brewer and maltster, who leased and owned malt houses and inns in Henley from the early 1750s, many in partnership with James Brooks. He ran the Brewery in Bell Street with Brooks and encouraged his nephew, Robert Brakspear to join him there in 1775. A leading figure in the town, he was Mayor of Henley on four occasions between 1762 and 1793. He was a partner in the bank Hayward, Fisher and Brakspear, established in Henley in 1791. In the 1793 Town Directory he was listed as 'gentry', showing that it was possible for a local merchant to rise to a position of standing in society.

A stone on the wall of a malt house in the Greys Road car park, engraved RJH 1778 may celebrate his development of a nearby property.

Henley in the Age of Enlightenment

Robert Brakspear

"An eminent brewer at Henley-on-Thames" – 'The Gentleman's Magazine', 1812.

Robert Brakspear (1750 – 1812) was born in Faringdon, the son of a tailor. At the age of 19 he became landlord of the Cross Keys in Witney, where he brewed beer to sell to other inns. From 1775 he frequently visited his uncle Richard Hayward. He eventually moved to Henley in 1779 to work with Hayward at the Bell Street brewery, where he became a partner in 1781. By 1803 he was the sole owner of the business, where he was an advocate of a scientific approach to the brewing process.

"Brewing is undoubtedly a chymical operation, yet very few are those of the Trade but are totally ignorant of that science, unconscious that their Art hath the least relation thereto."

'Treatise on Brewing' Robert Brakspear

After his uncle's retirement in 1783, Brakspear took control of the brewing operation himself, adopting an analytical approach to the process that was far in advance of his contemporaries. In his notebooks he states *"Extraordinary Effects sets us to enquire the cause, whilst enquiries lead to Knowledge"*. He made good use of scientific instruments, such as thermometers and hydrometers, to measure and keep particulars of each brew. Details of the ingredients and an assessment of the quality of each brew were noted in code form to ensure secrecy. His main product was the thick black porter, rather like a stout, that was popular in the 18th century, but he also experimented with an amber porter, anticipating a later change of fashion towards a lighter bitter ale.

Drawings in his notebooks show that he was interested in the use of a separate steam condenser to collect the vapour produced whilst boiling the wort at the beginning of the brewing process. It is possible that he may have been influenced by local knowledge of the pioneering work of Humphrey Gainsborough and General Conway's later investigations into furnace designs and the manufacture of coke.

Robert Brakspear became an important figure in the town and was Mayor of Henley in 1794 and 1804. His careful observation and recording of the details of each brew gave an understanding of the factors needed to brew good beer. His son W. H. Brakspear founded the family firm that continued to brew beer in Henley into the 21st century.

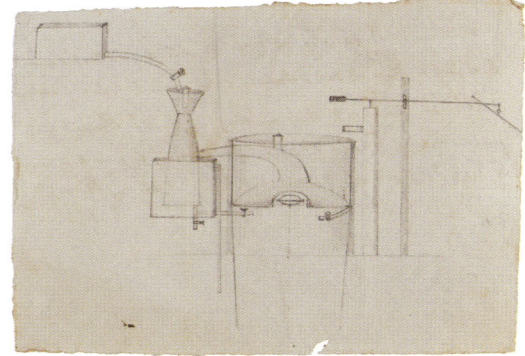

A sketch of a condenser by Brakspear with Patent notes on the reverse

People and Places

Thomas Hall and Harpsden Court

The Harpsden Court estate and the Lordship of the Manor of Harpsden had been in the Hall family since 1646, when it was purchased on behalf of Bartholomew Hall by his friend and fellow Middle Temple lawyer Bulstrode Whitelocke. Whitelocke was Lord of the Manor of Henley and may have felt that during the troubled times of the Civil War he would benefit from having a neighbour with similar Protestant sympathies. Though they attended the local church and avoided the persecution suffered by those who openly followed their nonconformist principles, the Hall family was reputed to have Presbyterian sympathies. They provided a safe meeting place for the local dissident Nonconformist congregation on their land during the late 17th century.

> "A fair ancient large manor place with dobil courtes and seven halls, including a Beggar's Hall. Thomas Hall inherited three sides of one court and demolished the wings (34 rooms)."
>
> 'Beauties of England and Wales', Vol. 12, 1813.

Thomas Hall (1720 – 1793) inherited the property from his father Bartholomew in 1747 and carried out improvements to the house. The old, mainly Elizabethan building was altered to incorporate a Music Room and Supper Room, exquisitely decorated with rococo plaster-work, for stylish social gatherings and musical evenings. Humphrey Gainsborough is said to have been responsible for the dome and the perfect cube proportions of the Music Room. The ceiling around the dome still incorporates four painted roundels featuring musical instruments, scientific apparatus and Christian symbols.

When the legislation against Nonconformists was relaxed, Thomas became a leading member of the Henley Independent congregation and his children were baptised in the chapel. His daughter Elizabeth married Samuel Allnutt, a Henley draper and brandy merchant, who was a member of the Independent congregation. Allnutt seems to have prospered sufficiently for him to be seen as acceptable to marry into the gentry and Elizabeth and her husband were buried in the Hall family vault at the chapel.

The magnificent plasterwork of the music room at Harpsden Court

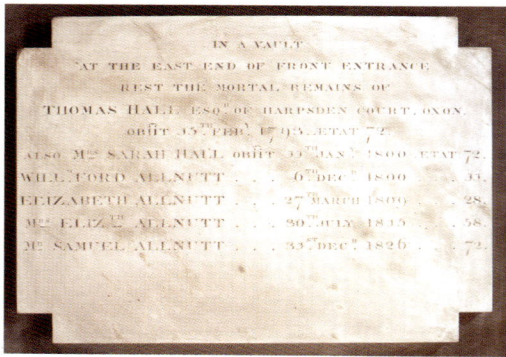

Independent Chapel at Rotherfield Greys

When Humphrey Gainsborough came to Henley in 1748/9 to take up the position of minister of the Independent congregation, the brick chapel on the outskirts of the town was only thirty years old.

The history of the Henley congregation in the area had followed a similar pattern to that experienced in many towns and villages across the country. During the Civil War and the Commonwealth, the overall authority of the Anglican Church had virtually collapsed and many church congregations came to value having control over their own approach to worship. When the authority of the Established Church was reinstated by the Act of Uniformity in 1662, many ministers were ejected from their livings for refusing to conform. This happened to the Rev. William Brice, Rector of Henley. Some members of his congregation, not wishing the affairs of their church to be governed by a remote central authority, followed him into exile from the Established Church. Persecution followed and

Interior of the old Chapel from a watercolour

A photograph of the old Chapel before its demolition in 1908

the dissident group, assisted by the Hall family of Harpsden Court, met in the woods at Harpsden. Probably by 1672, but certainly by 1685, the congregation was meeting regularly at a barn situated beside the Reading Road, owned by Bartholomew Hall of Harpsden Court. At that time, this barn was in the countryside within the parish of Rotherfield Greys and therefore was less likely to attract persecution, being outside the town boundary of Henley on Thames.

In 1689, when the Toleration Act at last gave Nonconformists the right to have their own preachers and places of worship, the barn finally became a legal meeting house. The congregation included many successful Henley freeholders and manufacturers. Their generosity enabled a brick chapel to be built in 1719 on land adjacent to the barn.

'The Orders of the Dissenting Church at Henley November 1st 1719' underlines their democratic approach to the running of the church and the very progressive attitude to membership. These are the surroundings in which Humphrey Gainsborough preached and cared for his flock for 28 years.

Humphrey Gainsborough

The Reverend Humphrey Gainsborough

Humphrey Gainsborough (1718 – 1776) was born in Sudbury, Suffolk, the son of a draper. Throughout his life he maintained a very close relationship with his younger brother, Thomas Gainsborough, the celebrated artist. They were both taken into the care of their uncle who left Humphrey twenty pounds a year to defray the costs of his training for the ministry. As a Nonconformist he was unable to attend an established University so he studied at the Congregational Fund Board Academy in Moorfields London, where John Eames, who was a friend of Isaac Newton, became his tutor. Newton's principles appear to have influenced many of his later engineering projects. In 1741 he married Mary Marshland (1711 – 1775) at St Anne & St Agnes Church, Aldersgate and then spent two years in Northampton, probably as assistant to Philip Doddridge, a leading Nonconformist teacher and preacher. He was appointed as minister of the Independent Chapel at Newport Pagnell in 1743. Five years later he became minister of the Independent Chapel on the outskirts of Henley on a stipend of £60 per annum, performing his first baptism on March 9th 1749.

John Wesley made notes in his 'Journal' of three visits to preach to congregations in Henley during Humphrey Gainsborough's ministry, but he does not mention him.

> *"Thursday November 10th 1768 – In the evening I preached in the Chapel at Henley to a considerable number of serious people. One or two of the baser sort made some noise, but I reproved them, and, for once, they were ashamed."*
>
> John Wesley's 'Journal'.

Humphrey was devoted to his wife, Mary, who supported him in his ministry. He was devastated when she died of cancer in 1775 and died soon after her. They are buried together at the chapel.

> *"one of the most ingenious men that ever lived, and one of the best that ever died... Perhaps of all the mechanical geniuses this or any nation has produced, Mr Gainsborough was the first."*
>
> Polyxena (Phillip Thicknesse) 'Gentleman's Magazine,' 1785.

There is a strong tradition that they lived in one of the cottages next to the chapel, but there is no firm evidence of this. This pair of cottages belonged to Peter Sarney, an affluent member of the congregation, during Humphrey's ministry. On Sarney's death in 1783, his executors who were all trustees of the church, sold the cottages to the church for £80 on condition that the property was to be used as *"a place of residence for the minister and his family"*. The cottages were later made into one house and are still used as the manse or residence for the present minister.

It is known that Humphrey was the occupant of 2 West Hill, Henley, in 1758, 1769 and 1775 and it seems probable that he was there during the intervening years. This would have given him a home in the midst of his congregation. He may have lived in one of Sarney's cottages prior to 1758, which could then have served as a study during the rest of his ministry.

Thomas Hall's great regard for the Reverend Humphrey Gainsborough is underlined by the fact that he commissioned a copy of a portrait of the minister from his younger brother Thomas Gainsborough, the well-known portrait artist. Hall is reputed to have been one of Humphrey's patrons, possibly allowing him workshop space at Harpsden Court.

The only records found so far of Humphrey's first ten years in Henley are of baptisms and burials at which he officiated, but by 1759 his engineering abilities were coming to the attention of members of the local gentry. Subsequent years saw his involvement in many engineering projects at their instigation.

Henley in the Age of Enlightenment

*Humphrey Gainsborough (1718-1776)
Posthumous portrait by his brother
Thomas Gainsborough
Commissioned by
Thomas Hall of Harpsden Court*

Humphrey Gainsborough

Inventions and Competitions

Sambrooke Freeman's regard for Humphrey Gainsborough was such that he planned to leave him £100 in his will, but it was never paid because he outlived Humphrey. In January 1759 Humphrey wrote to him as *"My good Benefactor"*, though there is no evidence of the precise nature of this relationship.

This letter details his ideas on *"making pendulums keep true time"* and it seems that Freeman encouraged him to communicate these thoughts to the Society of Arts. In April 1759 Humphrey duly wrote to the Society with his ideas on clock design, referring to his *"general Plan for helping the World to the Knowledge of true Time even at sea"*. Among other things, he suggested that a timekeeper would be more accurate if the pendulum was given its impulse at the mid point of its swing rather than at either end, putting forward the principle that came to be known as 'Detachment'. The discovery of this principle is usually credited to the French clockmaker Pierre le Roy (1717-1785), who described it to Louis XV in 1766. Le Roy did not publish his findings until 1770, so Humphrey Gainsborough's letter of 1759, still on the files of the Royal Society of Arts, indicates that he has the earliest claim to this discovery.

Through Sambrooke Freeman's influence, Humphrey became interested in competitions run by the Society of Arts for various industrial and agricultural designs. His model Tide Mill, making use of both the ebb and flow of the tide to drive the mill-stones efficiently, gained a prize of £60 in 1761, the equivalent of his annual stipend. No other entry was considered good enough to warrant a prize. On this occasion, he left an important part of his model, the 'false bottom', in Henley when he took it to London for the adjudication and had to make hurried arrangements to replace it before the judges' scrutiny took place. This gave rise to an accusation of cheating from a fellow competitor. Humphrey wrote desperately pleading the innocence of his actions. Samuel Norman, a Henley linen draper and a member of his congregation, supported his protestations to the panel of judges and they were assured of Humphrey's honesty. It is very unfortunate that only a brief description of this design has survived.

Humphrey Gainsborough's design for a Fish Wagon has survived in Sambrooke Freeman's family papers at the Gloucestershire Records Office. This was produced in 1762 in response to the Society's competition for a wagon to carry fish in good condition from the seaside to inland markets. It incorporated a pump mechanism operated by a balance beam that moved as the wagon's wheels bumped over the uneven road surface. This apparatus was supposed to blow air over the tiers of baskets loaded with fish and ice. He did not have time to make the model needed to enter the competition, but his drawing shows an ingenious device for keeping the fish ventilated on its journey. He was anxious that his idea should be available to the Society in case there were few entries for the competition. This is the only surviving detailed drawing of any of Humphrey's inventions.

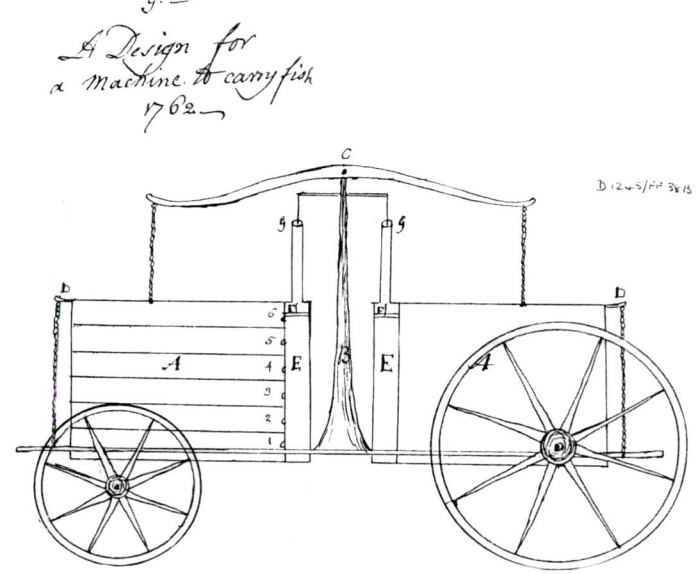

Henley in the Age of Enlightenment

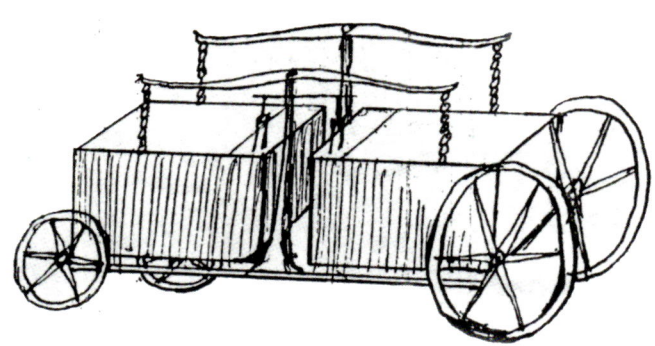

Sketch of fish wagon by Humphrey Gainsborough

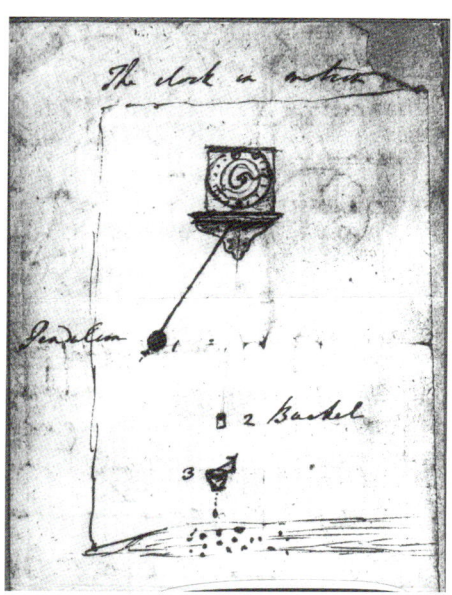

Drawing by Phillip Thicknesse of the gravity clock made by Humphrey Gainsborough and presented to the British Museum in 1788.

In 1765, the Society of Arts published a competition for the design of a drill plough in an effort to find a more effective way of planting and covering grass, corn and other seed than the old methods of sowing by hand that were still in general use. Humphrey's drill plough incorporated some innovative ideas and gained him the first prize and an award of £30. The panel of judges stated that *"the Principles on which the same is constructed are entirely new"*. A letter from the Reverend Thomas Powys, the Rector of Fawley and later Dean of Canterbury, supported his submission and indicated that the two had worked closely together for some time despite the difference in their religious philosophies. Only a brief description of Humphrey's design survives in the archives of the Royal Society of Arts. In January 1766, he was given leave to take his drill plough back to Henley for refurbishment prior to its display in the Society of Arts' collection. Unfortunately this collection was dispersed in the 19th century and there is no trace of its whereabouts.

During the early 1770s Gainsborough started to design a clock driven by small lead balls, which gave impetus to the clock as they fell. He planned to invent a means of returning the balls automatically to the top of the clock, however it is unlikely that he could have been successful. Another of his inventions was a sundial that would tell the time to the second. Philip Thicknesse, patron of his brother Thomas Gainsborough, presented both the gravity clock and the sundial to the British Museum after his death, but neither has survived.

Humphrey Gainsborough's signature from a letter to Sambrooke Freeman.

"Mr. Gainsborough of Henley, Oxon……..has made Simplicity and Cheapness the chief objects of his Attention, the most ordinary Workmen have skill enough to make it and the most ordinary Ploughmen have skill enough to use it."
Extract from the Rev. Thomas Powys' letter to the Society of Arts, 3rd December 1765 concerning Gainsborough's drill plough.

Humphrey Gainsborough

Bridges, Roads and Hydraulics

In 1763 as part of his landscaping plan for Park Place estate, Conway decided to build a rustic bridge to take the Henley to Wargrave road over the Happy Valley that led down from the house to the River Thames. William Pitt's brother designed the bridge, using stones from the ruins of Reading Abbey, but the structural engineering was carried out by Humphrey Gainsborough. This bridge still survives and carries much heavier traffic on the Henley to Wargrave road than could have been envisaged in 1763.

The approach to Henley from Maidenhead and London entailed negotiating the steep slope of White Hill. Many carriages and wagons took the less steep but longer route through the grounds of Park Place to avoid this hazard. In 1768, probably at Conway's instigation, Gainsborough was involved in the massive task of reducing the slope on White Hill by removing earth from the top of the hill to form a ramp at the bottom. He devised a system of ropes and pulleys to pull empty carts up the slope by making use of the weight of the loaded carts going downhill. A first hand description of this system was given by James Boswell, testifying to Gainsborough's involvement:

"29 March 1768...

At Henley we came out and went and looked at the machine with which they are levelling a very steep hill on the London side, by digging it down and throwing the earth into the hollow at the bottom. This is done without horses, by two carts which are contrived to work as buckets in a well. There is a road cut down the hill, they having begun at the foot of it, and cut upwards as they removed the earth. A number of men dig the earth and throw it into the cart, to which a strong rope is fixed, which is wound upon a horizontal wheel above the face of the hill yet entire. The moment the cart is full, a bell is rung to warn the man at the bottom of the hill, who then lets go the cart which he has emptied into the hollow. Then two men go, one on each side of the loaded cart (or but one for each cart, I forget which. I now recollect the two men on each side of the loaded cart only set it a-going), for a little way and push it along; then one returns to his companions, and one goes along with the cart, guiding it till he gets to the top of the steep bottom; then he has a long piece of wood fixed to the cart, but so as to be twisted about. This he twists till he fixes the end of it between two spokes of the left wheel, and so stops the cart.

In the meantime the weight of the loaded cart going down the hill pulls up the empty cart, which is filled, and then pulls up the other. The wheel to which the rope is fixed is so made as not to turn too quickly; so lets down the cart at a moderate pace. At three or four different places there are across the road double horizontal trees, or long pieces of wood, which are fixed by swinging ligatures or insertions in notches to a post. Upon these trees the rope is put to preserve it from trailing and being rubbed on the hill. The man who guides each cart runs now and then a little before it. He who goes down runs to draw out the tree on one side to receive the rope. He who goes up runs to draw out the tree to receive the rope on the other side; and as the one side is drawn out, the other falls in, and it is so contrived that by these means the ropes are always kept at a proper elevation. This method was invented lately by a Dissenting clergyman at Henley. It is exceedingly useful, by making that be done by two men which would require a great number of horses and oxen."

From: 'Boswell in Search of a Wife 1766 – 1769' edited by Frank Brady and Frederick Pettle (Heinemann 1957).

The Henley Coach crossing the bridge outside The Angel on its way to climb White Hill, c1793. The coach ran from the White Hart Inn, Henley to Piccadilly, London.

Henley in the Age of Enlightenment

The decision to charge wagons by weight rather than size on the local turnpikes brought the necessity to provide evidence of load weights at tollgates. In 1766, Henley Town Council decided to construct a weighing engine, capable of weighing loaded grain wagons. They positioned it outside the Catharine Wheel in Hart Street, where corn merchants could also use it on market days. The Council had no hesitation in asking Humphrey Gainsborough to design and supervise the building of the machine and for this he was paid five guineas.

The report does not indicate whether the new cement was invented by Humphrey Gainsborough himself, but it shows that he was in touch with the latest developments in this field. Lord Charles Spencer was a politician and thus probably well known to Conway and Freeman. They presumably had sufficient confidence in Humphrey to recommend his services to their acquaintances. Wheatfield House was destroyed by fire in 1814 and no evidence of Gainsborough's device remains on the site. Humphrey's friend Richard Edgeworth, the inventor, indicates in his autobiography ('Memoirs of R.L.Edgeworth', 1820 p158), that he was responsible for a number of water supply schemes to estates in the country, but Wheatfield is the only site for which there is direct evidence.

Hydraulic Engineering

The Bath Chronicle of January 16th 1772 records:

"Lately was compleated, under the direction of the Rev. Mr Gainsborough of Henley, a most singular and curious performance in hydraulics, by which the seat of the Right Hon. Lord Charles Spencer, at Wheatfield in Oxfordshire, is supplied with water from a spring almost a mile distant:" The report goes on to say "The water forces itself up a hill in the way, which is done by means of a small copper bucket, working over a single pulley, that, by no other help than the weight of water, is constantly carrying itself up and down, filling below, and above emptying into a cistern, from which it passes to the house...............What is extraordinary, the pipes of conveyance are terra cotta united by a new invented cement, which renders them capable of being forced immediately after being laid, though it is used cold. The quantity of water given every day and night is at least 4488 gallons."

> "As many parts of the high land in the neighbourhood of Henley were ill supplied with water, every contrivance that promised to facilitate the means of raising it, were eagerly adopted This induced Mr Gainsborough to turn his thoughts to this subject. His inventive faculty might have been applied more advantageously, for it must be obvious, even to those who are slightly conversant with mechanics, that no possible application of the powers of men or animals can alter their effect in any considerable degree, and that the approach of wind is too variable, and of steam commonly too complicated for domestic purposes. He, notwithstanding, erected several ingenious hydraulic machines in various parts of the country, which showed a fertile invention, and in all their parts, a sound knowledge of the principles of mechanics. In many instances, he gave a large scope to his genius in obviating local difficulties and inventing tools to execute his purpose in country places where he could not enjoy the resources of the Capital."

Humphrey Gainsborough

River Navigation

In 1770 there was a plan to by-pass the River Thames from Maidenhead to Caversham with a more easily navigable canal. In response, the Thames Commissioners decided that the long overdue replacement of the hazardous flash locks near Henley with double gated pound locks had to be carried out as soon as possible. With Conway, Freeman and Powys as Commissioners it is not surprising that Humphrey Gainsborough was asked to oversee the construction of eight locks at Boulter's Lock (Maidenhead), Marlow, Temple, New (Hurley), Hambleden, Marsh Mills, Shiplake and Sonning. The principles upon which pound locks operated were well known by this time, but Gainsborough's skills would have been vital in fitting the new locks into the most appropriate positions at the chosen sites.

Detail of barge being winched against the current through the flash lock at Marsh Mills from Jan Siberechts' painting of 1698.

Henley in the Age of Enlightenment

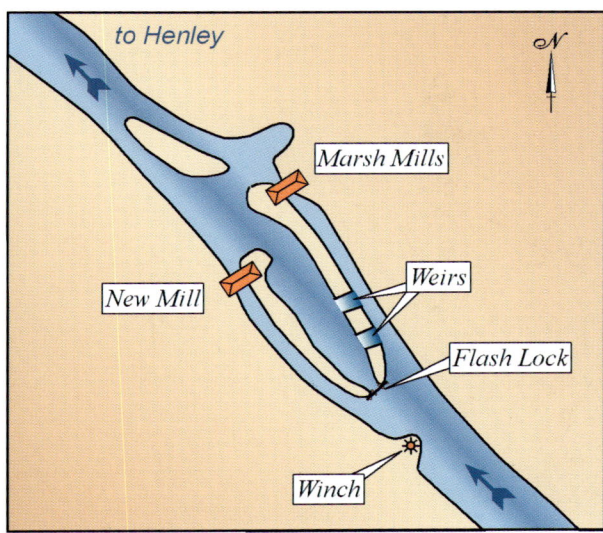

*Marsh Flash Lock, Henley
from a survey by Wm. Brasier, 1726*

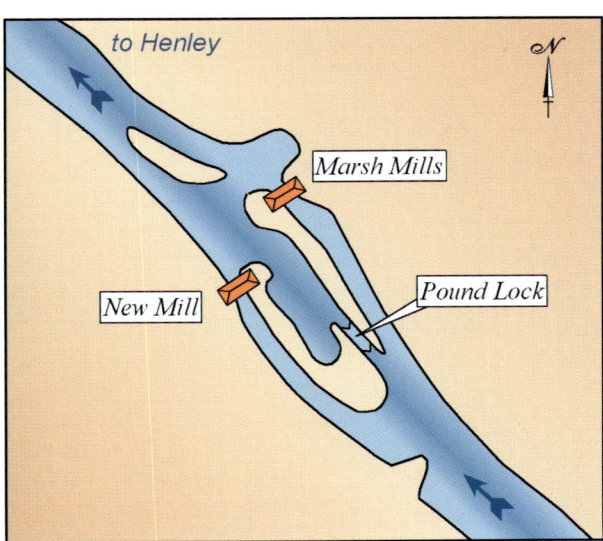

*Marsh Pound Lock, Henley
from the Fawley Court Estate Map, 1786*

After their completion, Humphrey was given the role of collecting the toll money from the local lock keepers. Perhaps to safeguard the large sums that might accumulate, he is reputed to have designed and made the ingenious security chain that is still attached to the door of the Manse.

He may have also designed a fire-resisting safe to provide a secure storage place for the tolls and Church documents. Two boxes still exist in Henley and a larger version has recently been found in Sudbury, the town where Gainsborough was born. The boxes are made of cast iron and their hinged lids are a remarkably good fit with the front and side walls. They are thought to be the first fire-resisting boxes invented and manufactured and one was successfully tested in a fire. The first grant of Letters Patent for such a safe was given to Richard Scott in 1801. Again, Humphrey appears to have been ahead of his time.

Humphrey Gainsborough

Did James Watt design the first working Separate Condenser ?

> *"Herein is W(att)'s greatest improvement, which was invented by one Gainsborough a dissenting minister, but secur'd by Mr Watt, so Mr G who is since dead, told my father, when he visited him at Henley-on-Thames."* Letter from Jonathan Hornblower (1753-1815) a steam engineer of Penryn, Cornwall, to his uncle Josiah Hornblower (1729-1809) from Transactions of the Newcomen Society.

Towards the end of his life, Humphrey Gainsborough worked on developing an efficient steam engine. His design was highly praised by Cornish mining engineers looking for improved water pumping engines. He made a model of an engine incorporating a separate condenser, an invention usually assigned to James Watt. On 6th February 1775, confident that his design was different from that of Watt's patent of 1769 and supported by Conway; Gainsborough entered a petition for a patent for his invention. It was described as *"a steam engine upon a new construction much more useful to the public than the common steam engine, by having much greater power and velocity"*.
'State Papers, Domestic Entry Book' Vol. 265, p355

Watt filed a caveat against the granting of this patent and seventeen days later petitioned to extend his own patent. Humphrey, convinced that his design was different, did not contest the caveat. Watt's caveat meant that Gainsborough's patent could not be granted until the Solicitor General was satisfied that his invention was indeed different from Watt's, or until the caveat had been withdrawn. James Watt wrote to Gainsborough to arrange a meeting in London to discuss the situation:

> *"I am sorry to have had occasion to give you this trouble, but judged it better for both parties that the matter should be cleared up now than to be left to be the source of lawsuits afterwards, as might be the case if the inventions clash with one another, as I hope they do not."*

By this time Humphrey's wife was seriously ill and, though certain that his design was unique, he decided to nurse his wife through her last illness rather than go to London to meet Watt, writing to him on May 16th 1775:

> *"Those who know both inventions have assured me that mine is totally different from yours. I must therefore leave you to act at your pleasure at the Patent Office, especially as it is impossible for me to be in town at present, and when God only knows, both I and Mrs Gainsborough being very ill. As you have been ungenteel enough to give me unnecessary trouble, I am only sorry that I did not endeavour to hinder your Bill passing in any form, which I have good reason to believe would have been in my power. However, I wish you success so far as your invention can go, being well persuaded it will do me no harm, it having once been my own, but was for many reasons given up for that which I am now upon."*

Gainsborough evidently believed that he had progressed beyond Watt's invention, but again in 1776 he was unable to make the journey to London this time because of his own illness. As late as August 1st 1776 he wrote to propose a meeting at a specified date and time with Watt's partner, Matthew Boulton, *"when I make no doubt but I shall easily convince you that my Invention is totally different from Mr Watt"*. His death occurred three weeks later but if this meeting took place, it would have had no influence on the patent situation. James Watt was granted a highly profitable extension to his original patent. Watt had experienced problems with both design and finance, which had caused him to suspend work on his 1769 patent for 5 years, but at Boulton's instigation, he applied for this extension. What these design problems were is not known, but they seem to have involved difficulties with the method of the packing of the piston. Humphrey Gainsborough had apparently overcome this problem since Boulton wrote to Watt in May 1775 that he wished they knew *"how Gainsborough packed his piston"*.

James Watt (1736 - 1819) first investigated steam engines whilst employed as mathematical instrument maker to the University of Glasgow. He patented the idea of using a separate condenser in 1769, but problems delayed construction of the engine. It was not until Matthew Boulton, a factory owner from Birmingham, joined him in partnership in 1774 that work on the engine resumed. By November 1776, a pumping engine with a separate condenser was working successfully.

industrial espionage enabled Watt to put right the problems with his own design. After Gainsborough died in 1776, the model steam engine remained for a while in the garden of his house in Henley. Thomas Gainsborough, his executor, was offered £1,000 for it by Cornish engineers but did not act and the model rusted away. Philip Thicknesse, Thomas's patron, wrote in his 'Sketch of Thomas Gainsborough's Life'.

"That engine alone would have furnished a fortune to all the Gainsboroughs and their descendants, had not that unsuspicious, good hearted man (Humphrey Gainsborough) let a cunning design artist see it ".

What is clear is that Humphrey innocently allowed a design engineer associated with Boulton to see his model. This act of

> Early development of the steam engine was directed towards finding an efficient way to pump water from flooded mine shafts.
>
> Thomas Savory patented an *"engine to raise water by fire"* in 1698. This filled a tank with steam, condensed it by chilling the tank, and used the vacuum created to raise water from a shallow depth. A new input of high pressure steam into the tank pushed the water to a higher level. This could only be used on shallow workings. At this time, high pressure boilers were extremely dangerous.
>
> Thomas Newcomen (1663-1729) patented his 'Atmosphere Engine' in 1705. This consisted of a beam, heavier at one end than the other, with a piston, attached to the lighter end, which was pulled downwards by the vacuum created by cooling low pressure steam beneath it in the cylinder. The piston was raised by an input of fresh steam aided by the action of the heavy end of the beam. This continuing cycle enabled a pump to be powered by the oscillation of the heavy end of the beam. Cooling the cylinder to condense the steam was time consuming and the whole process was very inefficient.
>
> James Watt's patent of 1769 proposed a separate vessel in which the steam could be condensed, enabling the piston cylinder to remain hot and the condenser to remain cool so that the efficiency of the pumping action was greatly increased. In partnership with Boulton, Watt developed a more effective rotary engine that was widely used in the mills and factories of the Industrial Revolution.

Humphrey Gainsborough – the man and the inventor

The young Humphrey Gainsborough by his brother Thomas

Details of Gainsborough's inventions and engineering projects testify to the fact that he was a very practical man with a mind capable of original thought, but there is little evidence of his character. It is, however, possible to make some inferences from his interactions with others, his few surviving letters and the tributes to him after his death.

The writer of Thomas Gainsborough's obituary in the 'Gentleman's Magazine' of 1788 (Vol 58) said of him:

> *"Mr (Thomas) Gainsborough had a brother, who was a dissenting minister at Henley upon Thames, and possessed as strong a genius for mechanics as the artist had for painting."*

This ability was recognised by his local patrons in a variety of ways. Sambrooke Freeman showed his regard for Humphrey by leaving him £100 in his will, a sum similar to that left to a life-long devoted servant. Thomas Hall commissioned artist Thomas Gainsborough to copy a portrait of Humphrey for him. General Conway supported his application for a patent for his steam engine in Parliament, perhaps trying to encourage this very modest man to claim some credit for his discoveries. In each case there is an implication that they are appreciating some other aspect of his character than simply his engineering genius. The obituary of Thomas has more to say about Humphrey:

> *"Few men were ever more respected than this worthy Divine; he was as eminent for humanity, simplicity, and integrity, as he was for genius."*

The Independent minister and teacher Doddridge at Northampton said that Humphrey was a *"thorough Calvinist"* and this is borne out by his desire to work for the good of mankind and not for his own advantage. This conviction comes out clearly in his letter to the Society of Arts on 5th April 1759 where he speaks of:

> *"my general Plan for helping the World to the knowledge of true Time, even at Sea."*

With many of his projects his aim was to solve a problem and he showed no interest in commercialising any invention that he produced in the process. The revolutionary drill plough and the fire-proof box are examples of this. Richard Edgeworth, in his 'Memoirs' relates that Humphrey was happy for others to use his ideas.

> *"I believe I took from him hints for some small contrivances which I have since executed, but, were he alive, he would not complain."*

The steam engine appears to have been developed in response to the requirement of Cornish mining engineers to obtain more efficient pumping equipment to keep their mine shafts dry. This was the only occasion on which he sought a patent. Perhaps Conway, who later applied for two patents for his own inventions, inspired this uncharacteristic behaviour. Humphrey, however, was not prepared to pursue the patent at all costs and refused to leave the bedside of his sick wife to defend his application against the objections of Boulton and Watt:

> "His wife had a cancer on her breast; and such was his affection and care for her, that, lest she should want his spiritual and corporal assistance, he would not quit either her apartment or her bed; the consequence was that it proved fatal to both."
> Polyxena (Phillip Thicknesse) 14th November 1785

As part of his desire to help mankind he was always ready to discuss his ideas and was sometimes naïve about the motives of those seeking advice. This caused problems when he was accused of adapting his tide mill model after it had been submitted, as a result of discussing it with one of his scheming competitors. Further problems occurred when Humphrey was prepared to discuss his steam engine model with an apparently interested designer who was, in fact, an industrial spy sent by Matthew Boulton. The secret that made Humphrey's separate condenser work efficiently was then, so it is said, conveyed to Boulton and Watt and incorporated in their design.

His considerable involvement in projects does not seem to have detracted from his duty to his congregation. There is no doubt that if he had been in any way lax in his ministry the democratic way in which the church was run would have resulted in a reprimand or even dismissal. Two ministers were persuaded to resign in the early 19th century: Nathaniel Scholefield in 1806 for incompetence, and James Churchill in 1813 because his authoritarian approach was not acceptable. All the evidence is that Humphrey was a highly respected and much loved minister who was devoted to his congregation. This is evident from the tribute written by Phillip Thicknesse and published in the 'Gentleman's Magazine' of 14th November 1785:

> "His genius as a man, his piety as a Christian, and his universal philanthropy was such that at Henley, where he was known, he was universally beloved and respected, and some men, of high rank in the neighbourhood, offered him very good preferment in the Established Church, if he would have taken ordination; but nothing could prevail upon him to leave his own little flock."

He would have been very embarrassed by such a tribute, but it seems to sum him up perfectly.

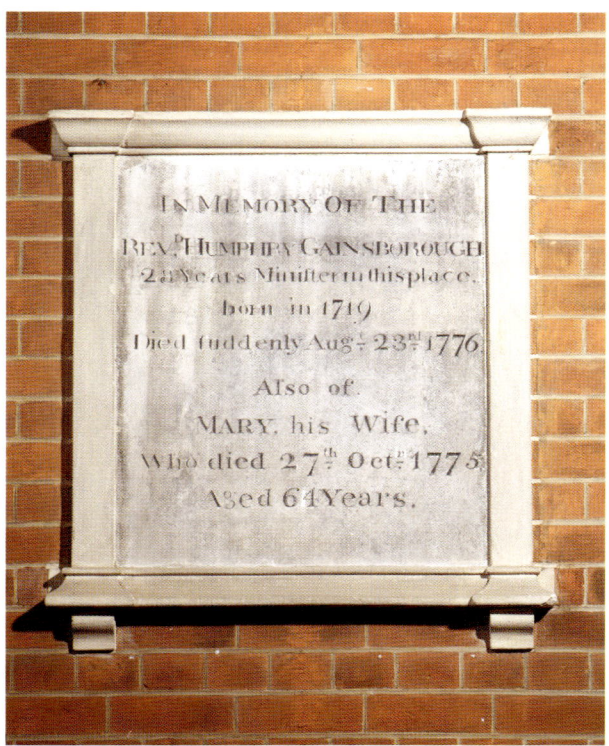

Memorial plaque at Christ Church United Reformed Church, Henley.

Diaries and Receipts

A first hand account of daily life

We are fortunate to have a unique insight into the Henley social scene of the late 18th century through the diaries, letters and sketchbooks of Caroline Powys of Hardwick. She was the wife of Philip Lybbe Powys and is often referred to as Mrs Lybbe Powys. Caroline was a gentlewoman by birth and married a member of the landed gentry, so that her acceptance into local society was assured. Her status was further enhanced through her husband's brother, the Reverend Thomas Powys, Rector of Fawley. His cheerful disposition and closeness to the Royal family as chaplain to King George III, made him an essential figure at any social gathering. Caroline and Philip Lybbe Powys were consequently invited to the balls, dinner parties and other fashionable events that made up the social scene. She regularly visited Bath and London during 'the Season', and her artistic abilities were known to Queen Caroline. She was a compulsive diarist and her descriptions of people and places, together with her sketches of things that had particularly taken her fancy, give a first hand picture of the lives of the privileged classes at the time.

Portrait of Caroline Powys née Girle (1738-1817)

> *"Her diaries present an accurate picture of life, manners and customs of the upper class of the period."*
> 'Passages from the Diaries of Mrs. Lybbe Powys 1756-1808', Emily Climenson (1899).

Receipts for all purposes

Caroline's 'Receipt Book' includes household hints, medicines and cookery recipes collected or received from her friends and neighbours. They give an insight into her social circle, the people she met and the sort of topics that must have occurred in conversation. The medicinal receipts vary from cosmetic aids such as *"excellent lip salve"*, *"nice soap for nails"*, or *"nice paste for hands"*, to remedies for everyday ills such as *"the Queen's recipe for pain"*, *"horse radish muff for the headache"*, and *"eight saline drafts for the gravel"*. Remedies for more serious illnesses are given such as *"millipedes for sore throat or cancer of the breast"*. *"Cream for children's faces after smallpox"* is a reminder that inoculation against this defacing disease had only just begun. She notes in her diary on 7th November, 1797 *"The two girls at Hardwick Innoculated this week"*.

The useful hints cover a range of treatments for domestic accidents suggesting *"gin to get out spots and stains from linen"*, *"ways to take out stains of boiled tea"* and *"blacking for hearth"* to more genteel pastimes such as *"cement for shell work"*, and *"ways to preserve flowers"*. *"Mr Gainsborough's recipe for cleaning stained glass"* is mentioned, but we do not know if it was devised by Thomas or Humphrey. Caroline spent a considerable amount of time at Fawley Court and so there are receipts from both Mr and Mrs Freeman: *"Mrs Freeman's sealing wax varnish"* and Mr Freeman's recipe for *"cheap green paint"*. This would have been very useful, as this fashionable colour was usually a very expensive commodity.

The culinary recipes cover a range of typical 18th century dishes that would have been on the menu at grand dinners and supper parties. They include: *"Lady Ailesbury's currants – red or white – the last prettiest"*, *"Rich plumb pudding"*, *"most excellent custards"*, *"candy flowers"*, *"calves' feet jelly"* and *"to dress a hare"*.

Henley in the Age of Enlightenment

The Sketch Book

Caroline Powys was also a competent amateur artist, and seems to have spent many quiet hours drawing and painting small sketches of *"useful and decorative ideas"* seen on her travels. Sometimes she drew practical inventions such as the improved design for a duck house, but often they were decorative ideas like the pretty ribbons used to hang small paintings in a parlour. At least one day appears to have been spent in Mr Freeman's library where she copied illustrations of classical designs from a book.

Other observations relate to unusual furniture designs and fashionable garden follies including the Temple on the island in the Thames, the folly in the grounds of Fawley Court and Lady Ailesbury's menagerie on the hill above Park Place.

Far left: "Chair and Chimney piece of Mr. Walpole's, Strawberry Hill".

Above and left: "Chairback from Mr. Freeman's Island, 1776".
Copies of paintings from "a fine book of Mr. Freeman".
"Mr. Freeman's fossil cases at Fawley Court".

Diaries and Receipts

The Social Scene from Caroline Powys' Diary

The Powys family visited Bath each year during the season. Caroline's diaries give details not usually recorded including the duration of the journey. They left Fawley on 1st March 1798 and took two days on the journey to Bath. On the return journey on 13th April they *"set out from Bath by 7, got to Marlborough before 5 and lay at the Marlborough Arms"*. The next day they *"set out by 7, breakfasted at Speen-hill and got to Fawley by half past 4"*. In 1799 the journey was quicker *"4th April. We left Bath at half past 7 after having breakfast, we dined at Speen-hill, where our own chaise and horses met us and got to Hardwick to dinner about half past 4"*. These journeys were uneventful, but even short excursions from home could prove dangerous.

> *"1797, December 19th. We were robbed by a highwayman only 4 miles from Henley on ye Oxford road just at 3 o'clock. We hear the poor man was drown'd ye week after by trying to escape after having robbed a carriage through some water which was very deep. He behav'd very civilly and seem'd as he said very distressed."*

These diaries also detail the social round in Henley at the end of the 18th century. The first 'Henley Ball' took place on 7th October, 1797 and was followed by another on December 4th, but it is not clear whether this became a regular feature in the social programme. The 'Gentlemen's Club' met weekly at this time at Mr March's (The Red Lion), but obviously Caroline could give no indication of what happened at these meetings. In 1798, there are mentions of the 'Henley Play', with some performances being sponsored by local gentry. She does not say where the plays took place, but there had been a long tradition of strolling players performing at the Broad Gates Inn in the Market Place.

> *"1797, January 29th. Caroline and I met the Fawley Court Family at the Henley Play, all the Gentlemen came to the Farce, a very full house and better performances than one could have imagined. 'The Jew and the poor Soldier'.*
>
> *February 7th. We all went to the Henley Play bespoke by the Freemans, 'A Cure for the Heart' and 'The Prize', a very full house."*

Many of the local gentry had put much time and expense into designing their houses and grounds for entertainment on the grand scale, so dinner parties and balls were frequently held.

> *"1796*
> *July 18th   Mr and Miss Cooper of Bix to dinner*
> *August 2nd   We dined at Mr Groote's (Badgemore), with Mr & Mrs Stonor of Stonor and Mr Cooper, Bix.*
> *August 3rd   We dined at Mr West's, Culham Court.*
> *August 9th   Went to a water party at Mr West's, who had had dinner at Medmenham."*

Caroline talks of visits to most of the big houses in the area where she was a welcome guest. Mr and Mrs Strickland Freeman at Fawley Court, Mrs Sambrooke Freeman at Henley Park, the Conways at Park Place, and the Halls at Harpsden Court are frequently mentioned. She does not record a visit to Stonor, but the Stonor family are frequently listed as guests at dinner parties that she attends. Her diary entries start after the death of Humphrey Gainsborough, but she does note the presence of the Reverend Mr Scholefield, a later minister of the Independent Chapel, as a guest at some dinner parties.

She describes in detail some of the entertainments given by local gentry. On 3rd January 1799 she attended a Grand Ball given by Lady Malmesbury at Park Place. This was Caroline's first visit to the house since Lord Malmesbury had bought the estate and made alterations to the house. *"...so intimate had we been with Marshall Conway and Lady Ailesbury that it was really a painful sensation the Idea of visiting again Park Place"*. However, she was impressed with the changes.

Henley in the Age of Enlightenment

> "1799, January 3rd. On this evening Lady Malmesbury gave a Ball at Park Place. The Company was to be there at 9. There was 75 of us, about 17 couple of dancers; twenty-one in the house, ...cards in one room, and the dancing in the library; tea, orgeat, lemonade, cakes, &c., brought round every half hour.
> At one, supper was announced in the room out of the library, two tables the length of the eating room, forming a crescent at the upper end in the beau window. On this, every elegance was display'd, and set off to the greatest advantage by gilt-plate, glass lustres, and other ornaments."

Table set for second course

Grand Entertaining

The diaries often mention elegant evening parties at the large houses around Henley. Grand entertaining in a country house always included an enormous evening meal with more than twenty different dishes arranged in three courses. The guests gathered during the afternoon and might start eating as early as 4 o'clock, although during the 18th century fashionable dining was delayed into the early evening.

Table set for dessert

Typical Menu

First Course	Second Course of Roasted Meats
Green Pea Soup served by the Host	Hares and Rabbits from the Estate
	Jugged Pigeons
Boiled Turkey in Prune Sauce	Poultry
Stewed Venison	Goose
Oyster loaves	Potted Eels
Veal escalopes with lemon	Mock Brawn
Boiled Beef	Peacock Pie
Fried Savaloys	Potato Pudding
Fish Baked in Pastry Served when the soup tureen was removed	Note: Very few vegetables were eaten by the wealthy

Diaries and Receipts

A long interval of three hours or more was often taken between the second course and the dessert. When the guests returned to the table, it had been transformed with mirrors, candles and glassware. For special occasions ornate models of buildings or gardens were created from marzipan and sugar icing. Table centres of pyramids of candied fruit and marzipan shapes or sweetmeats were served with delicate sorbets and syllabubs in jelly glasses, puddings and fresh fruits from the kitchen garden and greenhouse. Trays of refreshing drinks and small cakes would be offered to sustain the guests until supper was served after midnight. The party would continue until breakfast and guests would return home in the safety of daylight. During the evening the company might listen to music, dance or play cards.

An event of this kind was the central feature of the Henley Gala in 1777, which was described by Mrs Powys.

The Henley Gala

In early January 1777 Lord Villiers of Phyllis Court staged a Gala Week for the local gentry and their friends with a grand ball on Wednesday, stage plays on Monday and Friday and supper parties.

Mr and Mrs Sambrooke Freeman held the grand ball at Fawley Court, with dancing in the saloon and two rooms set aside for the card games, loo, vingt-une, and whist. A sumptuous supper was served to ninetytwo people at 12.30am, after which dancing continued until nearly 6am. The Powys family were hardly up and breakfasted by 3pm the next day.

Two plays 'The Provok'd Husband' by Vanburgh and Cibber and 'Pygmalion' by Rousseau played to full houses in a 300 seat theatre fitted up by Lord Villiers in the stables of Mr Anthony Hodges' house at Bolney Court.

> Card games, usually played for money, were an important feature of society gatherings. Large sums of money could be lost, even driving some gamblers, such as John Damer, to suicide.
>
> Loo was a favourite gambling game, played with a normal pack of cards by up to eight players, each with a three or five card hand. Tarot was another popular gambling game, requiring a special pack of up to 97 cards, but at the end of the 18th century the cards began to be used for occult purposes and this use is now better known than the original games. Gaming tokens were used mainly at gaming houses to prevent disputes over settlement of debts at the table They were often primitive copies of the coin of the realm with added slogans or advertisements.

Typical 18th century Ball from 'The Comforts of Bath: Ball at the Upper Assembly Rooms' by Thomas Rowlandson

All the parts were played by local nobility and their friends and the Reverend Thomas Powys wrote a verse prologue for each play. The performances were followed by a supper and ball given by Lord Villiers at the Bell Inn in Henley, where dancing continued until 6 am. On the preceding Saturday a rehearsal of the plays took place before Mr Hodges' tenants and the many Henley townspeople who wished to attend.

On Friday night, one of the post-chaises taking passengers from the plays to the ball in Henley was held up by a highwayman in an unsuccessful attempt to steal diamonds worth £12,000, belonging to Lady Grandison. The jewels had been lent to Miss Hodges as part of her costume for the play.

List of those attending the Gala Ball

> **In the Play of 'The Provoked Husband'**
> **by Mr Vanburgh and Mr Cibber**
> **acted at Bolney Court, Oxon**
> **by permission of Anthony Hodges Esq.**
>
> The Part of Count Bosset will be played by
> Lord MALDEN
> The Part of Squire Richard will be played by
> Mr ONSLOW (son of Lord ONSLOW)
> The Part of Lord Townly will be played by
> Lord VILLIERS
> The Part of Lady Townly will be played by
> Miss HODGES
>
> Prompted by Mrs HOWE (sister of Lord HOWE),
> assisted by the Rev T. POWYS
>
> Prologue by the Rev. T. POWYS will be spoken by Lord VILLIERS
>
> **In the Play of 'Pygmalion'**
> **wrote in French by the famed Rousseau**
>
> The Part of the Prince will be played by the famous
> Monsieur TESSIER
> The Part of the Statue will be played by
> Miss HODGES
>
> Prologue by the Rev. T. POWYS will be spoken by Lord MALDEN

The Duke of Argyle	Lady Villiers	John Pitts family
Lord Frederick Cavendish	Lady Dowager	General Pitts family
Count Brule	Lady Tyrconnel	Howe family
Lord Tyrconnel	Lady Sefton	Pratt family
Lord Beauchamp	Lady Powys	Clayton family
Lord Harrowby	Lady Harrowby	Freeman family
Lord Sefton	Lady Almeria Carpenter	Price family
Lord Rivers	Lady Louisa Clayton	Tufnel family
Lord Camden	Lady Caroline Herbert	Vanderstegen family
Lord Macclesfield	Lady Harriot Herbert	Jennings family
Lord Barrymore	Lady Cecil Price	Rice family
Lord Parker	Lady M. Churchill	Morton family
General Conway	Lady Elizabeth Conway	Stonor family
Sir George Warren	Lady M. Parker	Tilson family
Sir Thomas Stapleton	Lady Isabella Conway	Englefield family
Sir Michael Fleming	Lady Warren	North family
Sir Harry Englefield	Lady Englefield	Monson family
Sir George Beaumont	Lady Cornwall	Winford family
Lady Grandison	Sir Thos Clarges	Herbert family
Lady Aylesbury	Onslow family	Eliot family
Lady Egremont	Churchill family	&c
Lady Hertford	Conway family	
Lady Macclesfield	Rivers family	

Mr Garrick (who was to have been there) was ill with gout.

Caroline Powys' list of those present at the Gala illustrates the established social standing of the gentry in the neighbourhood. Although they hosted the grand ball the untitled Freeman family are listed below the Lords, Knights and Ladies.

Social order was still firmly in place, although ideas, inventions and the arts were rapidly changing the 18th century prior to the Industrial Revolution.

Acknowledgements

All photography by Jaap Oepkes, except

pp 6, 21, 25 & 38 by Adrian Arbib,

p 5 River & Rowing Museum,

p 9 Jersey Heritage Trust,

p 12 Christies Images,

p 15 Dean and Chapter of Canterbury,

p 17 copyright Jarrold Publishing,

p 23 copyright British Museum

p 30 National Gallery of Ireland,

p 35 Fairfax House, York.

Design by Graffixx Consultancy

Index

Henley in the 18th Century	5
Prosperity and Politics	6
The Social Hierarchy	8
General Seymour Conway	10
Lady Caroline Ailesbury	12
Mrs Anne Seymour Damer	12
Sambrooke Freeman	14
The Reverend Thomas Powys	15
Thomas Stonor of Stonor Park	16
Anthony Hodges of Bolney Court	16
Richard Hayward	16
Robert Brakspear	17
Thomas Hall of Harpsden Court	18
The Independent Chapel at Rotherfield Greys	19
The Reverend Humphrey Gainsborough	20
Caroline Powys' Diary	32
The Henley Gala	36